Jokes For Pl

The Ultimate Collection of Plumbing Jokes

Published by Glowworm Press
7 Nuffield Way
Abingdon OX14 1RL
By Chester Croker

Plumbing Jokes

These jokes for plumbers will make you giggle. While we don't want to plug them too much, we hope you enjoy our collection of the very best plumber jokes and puns around.

We hope you don't feel we have plumbed the depths to bring you these funny plumbing gags which are guaranteed to get you laughing like a drain.

Disclaimer
All rights reserved. No part of this publication may be reproduced in any form or by any means without the written permission of the publisher. The information herein is offered for informational purposes only, and is universal as so. The presentation of the information is without contract or any type of guarantee assurance. Under no circumstances will any legal responsibility or blame be held against the author for any reparation, damages or monetary loss due to the information herein, either directly or indirectly.

FOREWORD

When I was asked to write a foreword to this book I was chuffed.

That is until I was told that I was the last resort by the author, Chester Croker, and that everyone else he had approached had said they couldn't do it!

I have known Chester for a number of years and his ability to create funny jokes is absolutely incredible. He is quick witted and an expert at crafting clever puns and amusing gags and I feel he is the ideal man to put together a joke book about our profession.

He will be glad you have bought this book, as he has an expensive lifestyle to maintain.

Enjoy!

Plumb Line

Table of Contents

Chapter 1: Introduction

Chapter 2: One Liner Plumber Jokes

Chapter 3: Question and Answer Plumber Jokes

Chapter 4: Short Plumber Jokes

Chapter 5: Longer Plumber Jokes

Chapter 6: Plumber Pick Up Lines

Chapter 7: Bumper Stickers for Plumbers

Chapter 1: Plumber Jokes

If you're looking for funny plumbing jokes you've certainly come to the right place.

Here you will find corny plumber jokes and cheesy plumber jokes that plumb new depths.

Some of them are old and some of them are new, and while we don't want to plug them too much, we hope you enjoy our collection of the very best plumber jokes and puns around.

We've got some great one-liners to start with, plenty of quick fire questions and answers themed gags, some story led jokes and as a bonus some corny and cheesy pick-up lines for plumbers.

This mixture of plumbing jokes will prove that plumbers have a good sense of humor.

Chapter 2: One Liner Plumber Jokes

A contented plumber finished with his woman this weekend. He said, "It's over Flo."

I'll admit to not being a very good plumber so when I tried to repair my toilet I just couldn't get a handle on it.

Is the collective noun for plumbers a flood of plumbers?

I was going to become a full time plumber, but I just couldn't take the plunge.

A clumsy plumber accidentally flooded an ice making factory.

It has now gone into liquidation.

A ham-fisted plumber struggled to replace a tight washer because he didn't want to faucet.

A plumber friend of mine gave me some great advice, saying I should put something away for a rainy day. I've gone for an umbrella.

Plumbing is the only profession where you'll hear your boss say, "Be sure your 'joints' have lots of 'dope' in them!"

If a surgeon had to remove a bowel using plumber's tools, it would be a gut-wrenching experience.

Did you hear about the miracle of the blind plumber?

He picked up a hammer and saw.

Yesterday, a plumber's wife asked him to pass her lipstick but he passed her a glue stick instead by mistake. She still isn't talking to him.

The blundering plumber tried to dislodge the obstruction with a thick-soled shoe, but he only succeeded in clogging up the drain.

Did you hear about the plumber who stole a calendar? He got twelve months.

A plumber is the only person who can take a leak while they fix a leak.

When I was younger my most successful chat up line was "Don't sleep with a drip. Call a plumber."

Plumbers are the only people on Earth that can feel good about being shitty.

Anybody who has any doubt about the ingenuity or the resourcefulness of a plumber never got a bill from one.

A plumber is the only man who can tell his customers that their crap is his family's bread and butter.

Porn gives people an unrealistic expectation of how quickly a plumber will come to your house.

Confucius says, "Man who dig for watch in toilet, bound to have shitty timing."

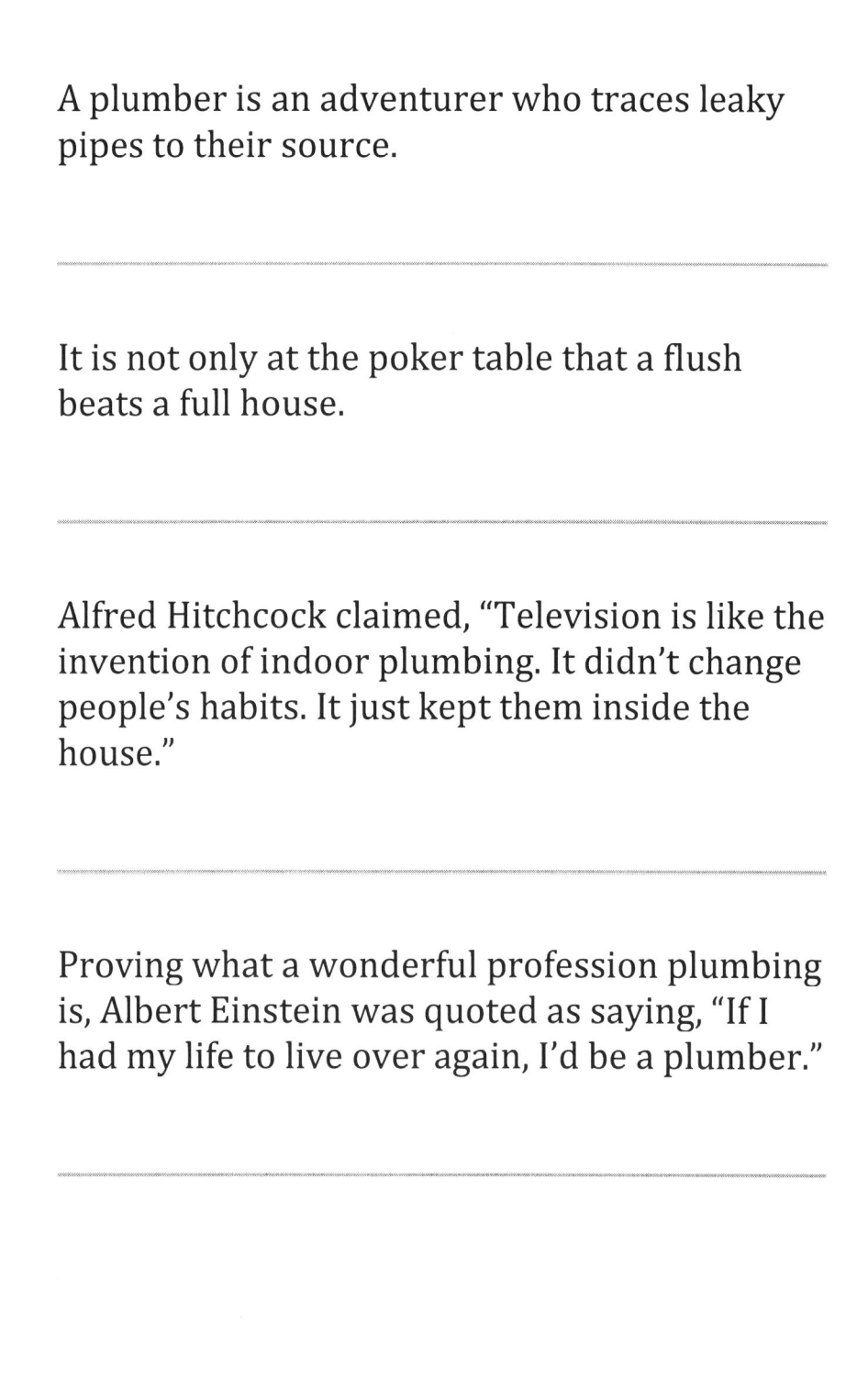

A plumber is an adventurer who traces leaky pipes to their source.

It is not only at the poker table that a flush beats a full house.

Alfred Hitchcock claimed, "Television is like the invention of indoor plumbing. It didn't change people's habits. It just kept them inside the house."

Proving what a wonderful profession plumbing is, Albert Einstein was quoted as saying, "If I had my life to live over again, I'd be a plumber."

Our apprentice plumber is learning to tap dance. He isn't very good though. He keeps falling in the sink.

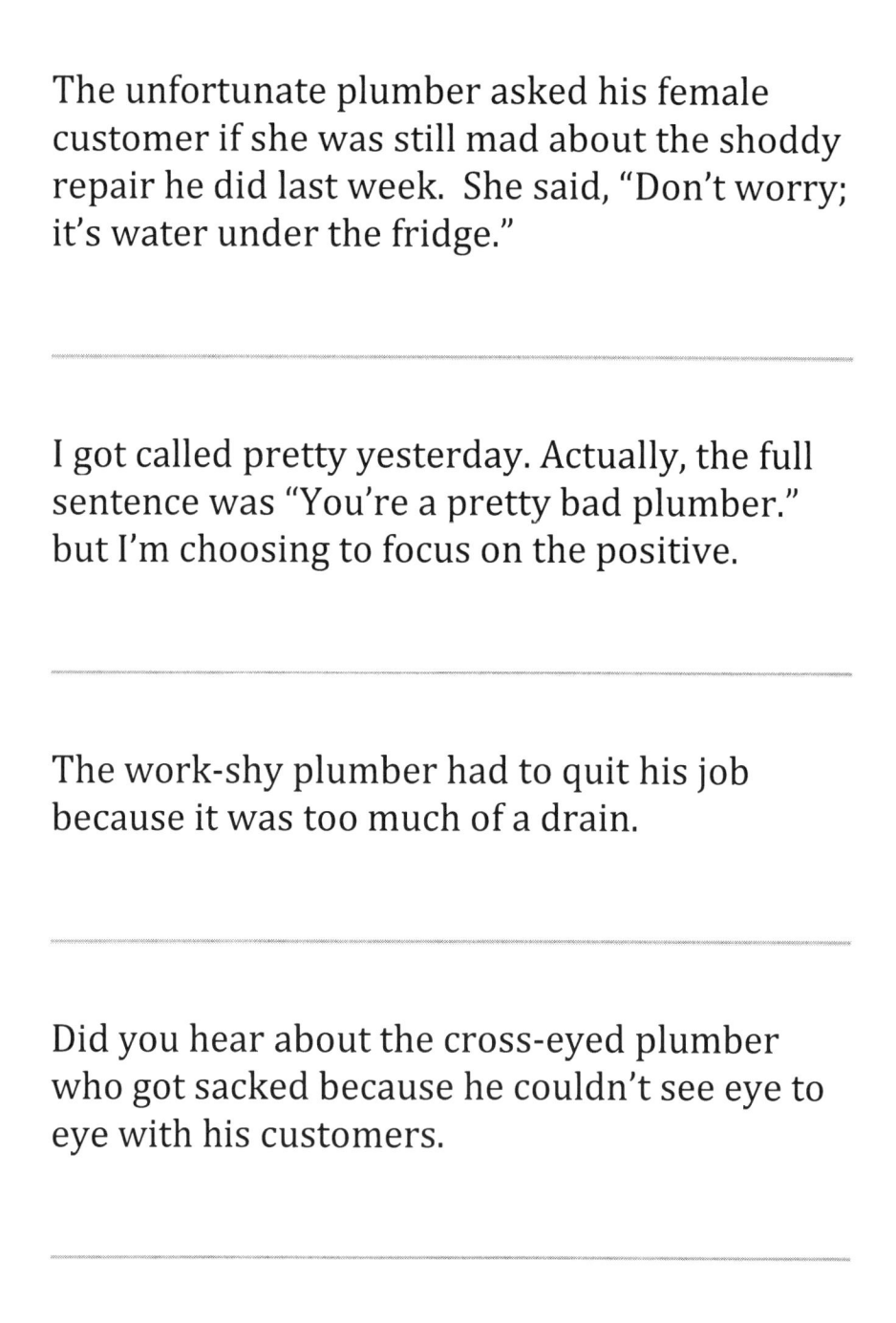

The unfortunate plumber asked his female customer if she was still mad about the shoddy repair he did last week. She said, "Don't worry; it's water under the fridge."

I got called pretty yesterday. Actually, the full sentence was "You're a pretty bad plumber." but I'm choosing to focus on the positive.

The work-shy plumber had to quit his job because it was too much of a drain.

Did you hear about the cross-eyed plumber who got sacked because he couldn't see eye to eye with his customers.

Before a plumber retires, he takes the final plunge.

Chapter 3: Q&A Plumber Jokes:

Q: Why are plumbers good at poker?
A: *They know how to get a royal flush.*

Q: What are a plumber's favorite shoes?
A: *Clogs.*

Q: Why did the plumber start dancing?
A: *He knew a little tap.*

Q: Why was the plumber depressed?
A: *His career went down the toilet.*

Q: Why did the plumber retire early?

A: *He was flushed with success!*

Q: What is a plumber's least favorite vegetable?
A: *A leek.*

Q: Why couldn't the plumber get a date?
A: *He was a real drip.*

Q: How are doctors and plumbers alike?
A: *They both bury their mistakes.*

Q: What do you call a fairy using the toilet?
A: *Stinker bell.*

Q: What kind of dreams does a plumber have?

A: *Pipe dreams!*

Q: How many plumbers does it take to change a light bulb?
A: *Three. A boss to tell a plumber, a plumber to tell his helper, a helper to get his electrician friend to do it.*

Q: Why does Australia need a lot of skilled plumbers?
A: *Because it is surrounded by water.*

Q: What's the one thing you'll never see a plumber do?
A: *Bite his nails.*

Q: How did the blind woman's parents punish her when she did something wrong?
A: *They stuck a plunger in the toilet.*

Q: What do you call a bathroom Superhero?

A: *Flush Gordon.*

Q: What did one toilet say to the other toilet?
A: *You look flushed.*

Q: What do you call a plumber who is happy every Monday morning?
A: *Retired.*

Q: Why don't blondes bring their iPhones into the bathroom?
A: *Because they don't want anyone stealing their IP address.*

Q: What's the difference between a doctor and a plumber?
A: *A doctor washes his hands **after** he has gone to the toilet.*

Q: Why did the plumber fall asleep at work?

A: *His job was draining.*

Q: Why doesn't Chuck Norris have to flush the toilet?
A: *He scares the shit out of it!*

Q: Why did they install a toilet at the garbage heap?
A: *Everyone had to take a dump.*

Q: What do you call a country where everyone is pissed?
A: *A urination.*

Q: Why was the plumber depressed?
A: *His career went down the toilet.*

Q: How are a body builder and a plumber alike?

A: *Both love pumping iron.*

Q: Why did the ant fall off the toilet seat?
A: *Because he was pissed off.*

Q: Why did the cannibal plumber get told off by his boss?
A: *For buttering up the customers.*

Q: What do plumbers say to their customers?
A: *Each time you flush a toilet, you put food in my family's mouth.*

Q: What would you find in Superman's bathroom?

A: *A Superbowl.*

Chapter 4: Short Plumber Jokes

A plumber called Paddy calls up his local paper and asks "How much would it be to put an ad in your paper?"

"Five dollars an inch," a woman replies. "What are you selling?"

"A ten-foot ladder," said Paddy before slamming the phone down.

A plumber is struggling to find a parking space.

"Lord," he prayed. "I can't stand this. If you open a space up for me, I swear I'll give up the booze and go to church every Sunday."

Suddenly, the clouds part and the sun shines onto an empty parking spot. Without any hesitation, the plumber says: "Never mind Lord, I found one."

Two plumbers are talking about sex. The first plumber says that he reckons sex is 75% work and 25% pleasure. The second plumber says he reckons sex is 25% work and 75% pleasure. Getting nowhere, they decide to ask their apprentice for his opinion.

"Sex is all pleasure" says the apprentice.

"Why on earth do you say that?" ask the plumbers.

The apprentice replies "Because if it there is any work involved, you two have me do it."

A dog walks into a pub, and sits down. He says to the barman, "I'd like a pint of lager and a packet of crisps please".

The barman says, "Wow, that's amazing - you should join the circus!'"

The dog replies, "Why? Do they need plumbers?"

This young plumber is sitting at the bar after work one night, when a big construction worker sits down next to him.

They drink a few beers together, and the conversation gets on to nuclear war.

The plumber asks the construction worker, "When you hear the sirens, and you know you've only got 15 minutes left to live, what would you do?"

The construction worker replies, "I am gonna make it with anything that moves."

The construction worker then asks the plumber what he would do to which he replies, "I'm going to try and keep completely still."

A plumber in my area went to jail for dealing drugs.

I've been one of his loyal customers for over ten years, and I had no clue he was a plumber.

A plumber tries to enter a bar wearing a shirt open at the collar, and he is met by a bouncer who tells him that he needs to wear a necktie to gain admission.

So the plumber goes to his car and tries to find a necktie but he can't find one.

However he knows he has some jump leads in his boot; and in desperation he ties these around his neck, and he manages to somehow make an acceptable looking knot and he lets the cable ends dangle free.

He goes back to the bar and the bouncer carefully looks him over, and then says to him, "Well, yes, you can come in - just don't start anything!"

An urgent call was put in for a plumber first thing in the morning but he didn't arrive until early evening.

"How is it?" he asked entering the house.

"Not too bad," replied the home owner. "While we were waiting for you to arrive I taught my wife how to swim."

The plumber complained to his friend that his wife doesn't satisfy him anymore.

His friend advised he find another woman on the side, pretty sharpish.

When they met up a month or so later, the plumber told his friend, "I took your advice. I managed to find two women on the side, yet my wife still doesn't satisfy me!"

I went to my boss at work and I said, "I need a raise. Three other companies are after me."

He said, "Really? Which other companies are after you?"

I replied, "The electric company, the gas company and the water company."

An old plumber was walking along the road one day when he came across a frog.

He reached down, picked the frog up, and started to put it in his pocket. As he did so, the frog said, "Kiss me on the lips and I'll turn into a beautiful woman and show you a really good time."

The old plumber carried on putting the frog in his pocket.

The frog said, "Didn't you hear what I said?"

The plumber looked at the frog and said, "Yes, but at my age I'd rather have a talking frog."

A plumber called Nigel and a roofer called Gary were working on a building site. Gary is up on the scaffolding on the first floor and somehow he accidentally cuts off his ear, and he yells down to Nigel "Hey, look out for my ear I just cut off."

Nigel looks around and calls up to Gary, "Is this your ear?"

Gary looks down and says, "Nope. Mine had a pencil behind it!"

A young plumber is in love with a girl and he goes to the girl's father to ask for her hand in marriage.

The father says "With the money you have, you can't even pay for my daughter's toilet paper."

The plumber replies, "Don't worry, I'm not going to marry a girl who is full of crap."

A local doctor calls his local plumber out in the middle of the night because his toilet had a blockage. He insisted that it was urgent and needed to be attended to immediately.

Upon arrival the plumber lifted the toilet lid, threw in two aspirins, and said, "If it's still there in the morning, give me another ring."

A proud father is showing pictures of his three sons to an old friend and he is asked "What do your boys do for a living?

He replied "Well my youngest is a neurosurgeon and my middle is a lawyer," He replied.

"What does the oldest child do?" his friend asked.

The reply came, "He's the plumber that paid for the others' education."

A Texan is admiring Niagara Falls. As the incredible amount of water crashes over the falls, a local walks up to the Texan and says, "I bet you don't have anything like that where you are from."

"We sure don't," admits the Texan, "But we have plumbers that can fix it."

The plumber was working in a house when the lady of the house said to him, "Would it be okay for me to take a bath while you're eating lunch?"

The plumber stopped working, sat on the toilet and replied, "It's okay with me lady, as long as you don't splash my sandwiches."

A plumber goes to the doctor with a hearing problem.

The doctor says, "Can you describe the symptoms to me?"

The plumber replies, "Yes. Homer is a fat yellow lazy man and his wife Marge is skinny with big blue hair."

A plumber took his cross-eyed dog to the vet.

The vet picked the dog up to examine him and said, "Sorry, I'm going to have to put him down."

The plumber said, "It's not that bad is it?"

The vet replied, "No, he's just very heavy."

There was a young plumber called Lee,

who was plumbing his girl with great glee,

She said stop your plumbing,

I think someone's coming,

Said the plumber, still plumbing, "It's me!"

A burglar has broken into our local Police station and stolen the toilet.

Right now the Police say they have nothing to go on.

A plumber was called to a surgeon's home to fix a leaking tap that had kept the surgeon awake late at night.

After a ten minute job the plumber demanded $150.

The surgeon exclaimed, "Good Gracious. I don't charge this amount even though I am a surgeon."

The plumber replied, "I didn't either, when I was a surgeon. That's why I switched to plumbing."

Chapter 5: Longer Plumber Jokes

Exact Words

The homeowner was delighted with the way the plumber had done all the work on his house. "You did a great job." he said and handed the man a cheque. "Also, in order to thank you, here's an extra 80 bucks to take the missus out to dinner."

Later that night, the doorbell rang and it was the plumber.

The homeowner asked him, "What's the matter, did you forget something?"

"Nope." replied the plumber, "I'm just here to take your missus out to dinner like you asked."

The Pearly Gates

A plumber dies in a fishing accident on his 40th birthday and finds himself greeted at the Pearly Gates by a brass band. Saint Peter runs over, shakes his hand and says "Congratulations!"

"Congratulations for what?" asks the plumber.

"We are celebrating the fact that you lived to be 100 years old." says Saint Peter.

"But that's not true," says the plumber. "I only lived to be forty."

"That's impossible," says Saint Peter, "we added up your time sheets!"

Reunion

A group of plumbers, all aged 40, discussed where they should meet for a reunion lunch. They agreed they would meet at a place called The Kings Arms because the barmaids had big breasts and wore short-skirts.

Ten years later, at age 50, the plumbers once again discussed where they should meet for lunch.

They agreed to meet at The Kings Arms because the food and service was good and there was an excellent beer selection.

Ten years later, at age 60, the friends again discussed where they should meet for lunch.

They agreed to meet at The Kings Arms because there were plenty of parking spaces, they could dine in peace and quiet, and it was good value for money.

Ten years later, at age 70, the friends discussed where they should meet for lunch.

They agreed to meet at The Kings Arms because the restaurant was wheelchair accessible and had a toilet for the disabled.

Ten years later, at age 80, the plumbers, now all retired, discussed where they should meet for lunch.

They agreed to meet at The Kings Arms because they had never been there before.

The Parrot and the Plumber

A plumber is called to the house of a cute little old lady. There is a restless Doberman sitting in the kitchen drooling and growling under his breath, and a parrot whistling contentedly next to him on his perch.

Half-way through the job, the little old lady tells him she's going to the grocery store. The plumber asks the little old lady if he'll be safe while she's away to which she smiles and says, "Oh yes! Frankie is so sweet. He wouldn't hurt a fly. He's a good doggie."

Then the old lady adds, "Oh. But whatever you do, do not say a word to the parrot."

Relieved, the plumber resumes his work. After the little old lady leaves, the parrot starts making a horrible racket and is calling the plumber all manner of rude names.

The plumber cannot concentrate on his work. Losing his temper, the plumber glares at the bird and screams, "Shut up, you annoying bird.", and goes back to his work.

There is silence for ten seconds; then the parrot squawks, "Stick it to him, Frankie!"

The Old Man

A young guy is driving his van when he sees an old man at the side of the road crying his eyes out. The younger guy stops and asks the old man what's the matter.

"I've had a great life," says the old man. "I was a successful plumber, and I sold my company to a large builder for plenty of money."

The guy says, "So what's the problem?"

The old man snuffles and says, "I built myself a huge mansion with a swimming pool!"

The guy looks puzzled and says, "Okay, so what's the problem?"

The old man wails and says, "I own a fast car."

The guy says, "I still don't get the problem."

The old man blows his nose and says, "Last month I got married to a 25 year old Playboy bunny."

The guy loses his temper. "Come on, old man – what is your problem?"

The old man sobs, "I can't remember where I live!"

Pulling Power

Carlo the property developer and his plumber buddy Pete, went bar-hopping every week together, and every week Carlo would go home with a woman while Pete went home alone.

One week Pete asked Carlo his secret to picking up women. "That's easy," said Carlo "When she asks you what you do for a living, don't tell her you're a plumber, just tell her you're a lawyer."

Later Pete is dancing with a woman when she leans in and asks him what he does for a living. "I'm a lawyer," says Pete. The woman smiles and asks, "Want to go back to my place? It's just around the corner." They go to her place, have some fun and an hour later, Pete is back in the pub telling Carlo about his success.

"I've only been a lawyer for an hour," Pete snickered, "And I've already screwed someone!"

Three Friends

Ron is chatting to two of his friends, Jim and Shamus.

Jim says, "I think my wife is having an affair with a plumber. The other day I came home and found a monkey wrench under our bed and it wasn't mine."

Shamus then confides, "Me too. I think my wife is having an affair with an electrician. The other day I found some wire cutters under the bed and they weren't mine."

Ron thinks for a minute and then says, "You know - I think my wife is having an affair with a horse."

Jim and Shamus look at him in disbelief.

Ron sees them looking at him and says, "No, seriously. The other day I came home early and found a jockey under our bed."

The Clean Floor

A team of plumbers was working outside my house.

I had just finished washing the floor when one of the plumbers asked to use the toilet.

With dismay I looked at his muddy boots and my newly polished floor.

"Just a minute," I said, "I'll put down some newspaper."

"That's all right, madam" he responded. "I'm house trained."

Train Passengers

A plumber, an electrician, a beautiful lady, and an old woman were on a train, sitting 2x2 facing each other.

The train went into a tunnel and when the carriage went completely dark, a "smack" was heard. When the train came out of the tunnel back into the light the electrician had a red hand print where he had been slapped on his face.

The old lady thought, "That plasterer must have groped the young lady in the dark and she slapped him."

The hottie thought, "That electrician must have tried to grope me, got the old lady by mistake, and she slapped him."

The electrician thought, "That plumber must have groped the hottie, she thought it was me, and slapped me."

The plumber sat there thinking, "I can't wait for another tunnel so I can slap that electrician again!"

The Professor

Note from author Chester Croker: This joke is really for mathematicians, but my publisher insisted I kept it in. I don't get the joke at all, but maybe you will!

A professor of mathematics had a leak in his kitchen sink so he called out a plumber. The plumber came the next day, sealed a few screws, and fixed the leak.

The professor was delighted. However, when the plumber gave him the bill, he was shocked. "This is one-third of my monthly salary!" he complained.

Well, all the same he paid the bill and then the plumber said to him, "I understand your position as a professor. Why don't you join our company as a trainee plumber? You will earn twice as much as you currently do. But do remember, when you apply, don't tell them your education level - they don't really like educated people."

So it happened. The professor got a job as a plumber and his earnings increased significantly.

One day, the boss of the plumbing company decided that every plumber needed to go to evening classes.

The first class was mathematics and the tutor, to check students' knowledge, asked the professor if he knew for the formula for the area of a circle.

The professor jumped up, but he realized that he had forgotten the formula. He started to reason it, and he filled the white board with integrals, differentials, and other advanced formulas to conclude the result he forgot. As a result, he got "minus pi times r square."

He was frustrated. He gave the class a frightened look and saw all the plumbers whisper: "Switch the limits of the integral!"

The Lawyer

On coming home from a late night at the office, the partner at a prestigious law firm discovered that his basement was flooded. He summoned a plumber. The plumber arrived soon afterwards, with a spare set of overalls and a cap that said "Blue Collar Guy".

The lawyer, still dressed in his expensive suit, silk tie, and gleaming wingtips, chuckled. "You're the first plumber I've met who has brought a change of clothes to a job."

The plumber smiled and went down into the basement, and the lawyer heard him working downstairs. Before too long, the plumber came back upstairs. "I'm almost done down there. I'm going to write up your bill, and then I'm going to go out to my van for a tool I need to finish up."

The plumber added, "The overalls and cap you asked me about, they're not for me. I'm looking for a new assistant, and I was hoping you might know somebody who wanted the job."

The lawyer responded, with more than a hint of condescension, "I'm a lawyer. Who would I know who would want to work as a plumber?"

The plumber shrugged, and handed the lawyer his bill.

A few minutes later, when the plumber returned from his van, he found the lawyer, dressed in the hat and overalls. "I had a chance to look over your bill while you were out," the lawyer said, "You have found yourself a new assistant!"

The Broken Leg

A plumber hobbles down the road with his leg in a cast and meets an old friend.

"How did you break your leg?" asked his friend.

"It's like this," he replied: "A customer had promised his wife that he would fix the sink plumbing on a particular day. That day, he realised he would need to stay late at work, so he called me. I stopped by the man's office for the house key, and went to work."

"When the wife got home, she saw my bottom half protruding from the sink cabinet. She assumed it was her husband, and proceeded to remove my trousers and give me some intimate attention, if you know what I mean."

Then the phone rang, and the woman left to answer it. When she returned, she angrily said, "That was my husband on the phone, so who are YOU?"

"I was startled, so when I got up to reply, I bumped my head and knocked myself out. The woman pulled me out, and must have fastened my trousers and called an ambulance."

"When the medics were carrying me out, they asked what had taken place – When I told them, they laughed so hard that they dropped me. That's when I broke my leg!"

The Washing Machine

A woman calls in a plumber when her washing machine breaks down. The plumber arrives, studies the machine, then produces a rubber hammer and gives it a hefty whack.

The washing machine starts working again and the plumber presents a bill for $200.

"Two hundred dollars?" says the woman. "All you did was hit it with the hammer."

So the plumber gives her an itemised bill:

Hitting washing machine with a hammer – $5.

Knowing where to hit it – $195.

Total - $200.

Union Plumber

A plumber was called to an upmarket house to repair a leaking pipe. Upon arriving, he found a luscious woman, who was dressed provocatively and was very flirty.

After a while, the two became extremely friendly and things got heated between them.

After an hour or two, the phone rang disturbing the bedroom shenanigans, and she hurried off to answer it, returning with the bad news that her husband was on his way home.

She said, "Tonight is his bowling night, so why don't you come back around 8 p.m. and we can take up where we left off."

The union plumber looked at the woman in disbelief. "What? On my own time?"

Three Daughters

A male plumber was talking to two of his friends about their teenage daughters.

The first friend says, "I was cleaning my daughter's room the other day and I found a pack of cigarettes. I didn't even know she smoked."

The second friend says, "That's nothing. I was cleaning my daughter's room the other day and I found a half full bottle of Vodka. I didn't even know she drank."

The plumber says, "That's nothing. I was cleaning my daughter's room the other day and I found a pack of condoms. I didn't even know she had a penis."

The Noisy Drunk

A drunk gets up from the bar and heads for the bathroom. A few minutes later, a loud, blood curdling scream is heard from the bathroom. A few minutes after that, another loud scream reverberates through the bar.

The barman goes into the bathroom to investigate why the drunk is screaming.

"What is all the screaming about in there? You're scaring the customers." he says.

"I'm just sitting here on the head and every time I try to flush, something comes up and squeezes my balls." replied the drunk.

So, the barman opens the door, looks in and says, "You idiot - You're sitting on the mop bucket."

The Train Ride

Three plumbers and three electricians are about to board a train to a convention. As they were standing in line for tickets, the electricians noticed that the plumbers bought only one ticket between them, and they ask the plumbers how they plan on getting to the convention.

"Watch and learn," one of the plumbers tells them. As soon as the train left the station, the three plumbers moved from their seats and they all squeezed into one restroom.

The ticket collector soon came through the carriage and knocked on the restroom door saying "Ticket please" The door was opened slightly and an arm reached out and one ticket was handed to the conductor.

The next day, the electricians decided to do the same thing so they only purchased one ticket between the three of them. However they noticed that the plumbers didn't purchase any tickets at all. They all boarded the train and as soon as the train left the station, the three electricians hurry for the restroom. A few moments later, one of the plumbers gets up from his seat, knocks on the restroom door and says, "Ticket please."

Chapter 6: Plumber Pick Up Lines

I have a dirty job. I'm a plumber.

Can I tinker with your pipes?

I am a professional pipe layer.

My plunger will bring out the colour in your eyes.

Come out with me and it will be all cisterns go.

I don't normally plunge into a relationship, but tonight I'll make an exception.

Are you a sucker for a man who knows how to use his equipment?

You're flooding my heart with emotions.

Tonight was going down the drain; until you walked in.

That's quite an elbow joint.

Plumber? I hardly even know her.

Want to see my plunger?

Let's become a potty of two tonight.

If there's anything I know how to do the right way, it's lay pipe. I'm happy to prove it to you.

You look like you could use a good plunging.

Want to flux?

I'd tap you.

I want to flush your pipes, baby.

Can I show you my plumbers crack?

Want to see my tool?

You make me feel flushed.

Don't sleep with a drip. Call a plumber.

Would you help me get this snake fully extended?

Baby, the love tap just keeps on gushing.

I've got a leak only you can fix.

Are you prepared to get wet, because these pipes are about to burst.

Chapter 7: Bumper Stickers For Plumbers

If you think its expensive hiring a good plumber; just try hiring a bad one.

Plumber by day. Pornstar by night.

Nobody puts a plumber in a corner.

Don't sleep with a drip – call a plumber.

Plumbers do it in the dark.

Chapter 8: Summary

Hey, that's pretty well it for this book. I hope you've enjoyed it.

I've written a few other joke books for other professions, and here are just a few sample jokes; these are from my electricians joke book:-

Q: What kind of van does an electrician drive?

A: A *Volts-wagon.*

Q: What do you call a Russian electrician?

A: *Switchitonanov.*

Q: What is the definition of a shock absorber?

A: *A careless electrician!*

Here are just a few gags from a book of mine unpretentiously titled 'The Punniest Joke Book Ever' which is available exclusively on Amazon:-

Trying to write with a broken pencil is pointless.

My wife has thrown me out because of my obsession with Arnold Schwarzenegger quotes. I told her, "I'll be back."

I was once engaged to a girl with a wooden leg, but she broke it off.

My grandad was half Irish, half Chinese. His name was Pat Noodle.

About the Author

Chester Croker has written many joke books and has been twice named Comedy Writer Of The Year by the International Jokers Guild. Chester, known to his friends as Chester the Jester, worked for a number of years in the building trade and came across many characters which provided him with plenty of material for this joke book.

If you see anything wrong, or you have a gag you would like to see included in the next edition of this book, please do so via the glowwormpress.com website.

He is on twitter @ChesterCroker if you want to follow him.

If you did enjoy the book, please leave a review on Amazon so that other plumbers can have a good laugh too.

Printed in Poland
by Amazon Fulfillment
Poland Sp. z o.o., Wrocław

66141666R00045